Dedicated to my one pure joy - Samuel

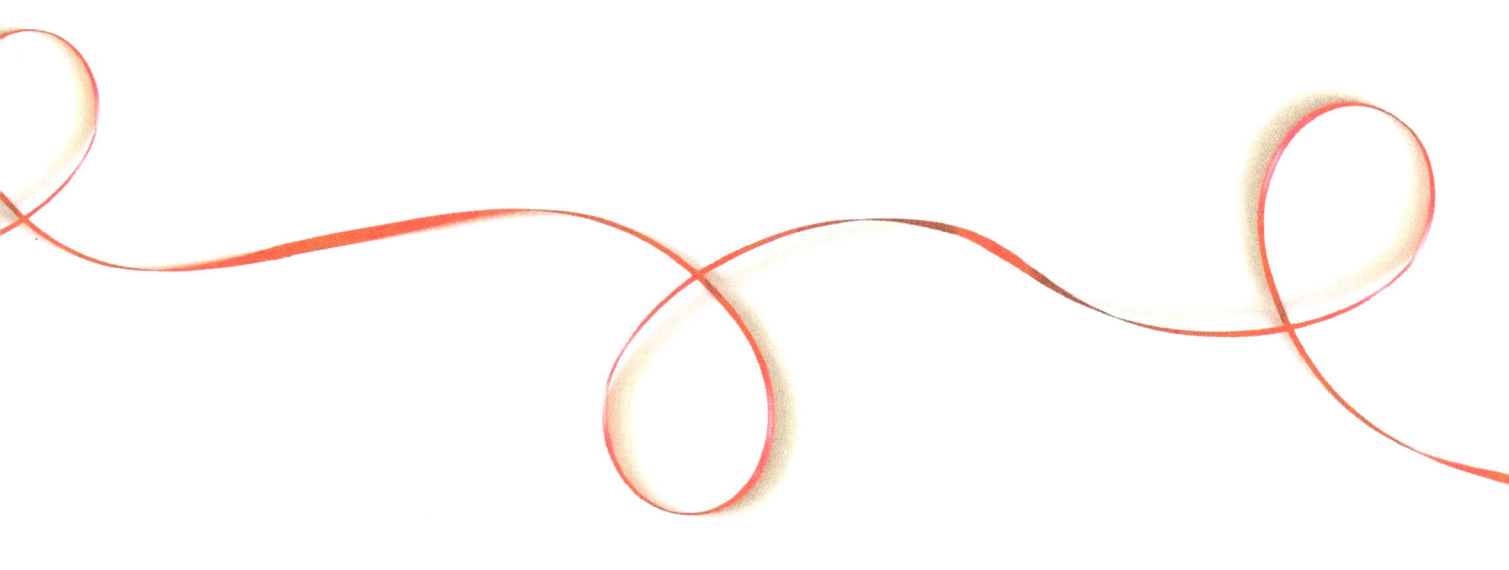

Copyright © Shirley Harvey 2016
All rights reserved. No part of this book may be reproduced, transmitted, or stored in an information retrieval system in any form or by any means, graphic, electronic, or mechanical, including photocopying, taping, and recording, without prior written permission from the publisher.

First edition 2016
ISBN 978-1-7750646-5-7
Published by Animal Publications in a magical place called Shirley World.
www.shirleyharvey.com

Written and Illustrated by Shirley Harvey

When sadness comes and visits awhile
There's a simple trick that will make you smile.
Just look in the mirror five times a day
And grin at yourself in a silly way.

The funniest thing I ever did see

Was a seal laughing in front of me.

There was nothing funny, nothing in sight

But stop he could not, try as he might.

When your body is heavy and weary
and your outlook on life is dreary,
there's a very good chance
that a move and a dance
will make you feel quite cheery.

Skip to the beat,

Skip with your feet,

Skip to the sound

As you pound on concrete.

Skip to the left,

Skip to the right,

Skip for the sun

Shining his light.

Skip for the moon

As she rests up high,

Skip like a loon

As you jump to the sky.

Care not for opinions

Or a disapproving glance

For happiness is yours

When you skip and prance.

I give you a gift
of infinite love,
of magical wishes
from stars up above.
I give you a gift
of my energy and time,
of a box of chocolates
or my second last dime.
I give you a gift
and it comes back tenfold
in the form of your smile,
worth way more than gold.

give

Sometimes the hardest thing to do
is receive a compliment or two.
You bat it away with a declaration.
"It's old," you say, without hesitation.
When you receive a gift and reply as such,
"You shouldn't have. I hope it's not much."
Remember that someone is giving to You,
so accept it with grace and say, "I thank you!"

Find a tree to sit yourself under,
stroke the grass and let your mind wander,
feel the earth beneath your toes
soaking up your worries, your woes.
Feel the sun warming your face,
feel a connection to this place:
The grass, the tree, the earth, the sound,
the smells, the colours, the treasures around.
A wonderful gift for you and me
is being in nature, under a tree.

Sometimes beauty is found where there's not.

With a shift of our glance to a different spot,

a change of our focus to something new

is all that it takes to change our view.

No matter how busy,

no matter the mess,

no matter your worries,

no matter your stress,

in the midst of your rushing,

in the midst of your day,

stop all your fussing

and take time to play.

The greatest joy is often found

in the darkest of times,

in the silence of sound.

When we lose the thing we most desire

and watch it leave,

flying higher and higher,

we have to let go, say goodbye

and trust that the universe

has a good reason why.

Although there are times when you feel all alone,
You can smile at a stranger or pick up the phone,
Hold a door open for someone in need,
Play with an animal or plant a seed,
Remembering that you are connected to all,
To plants and creatures, big and small,
To him, to her, to everyone,
To the moon, the stars, the earth, the sun.

With a wriggle and a whirl
And a giggle and a twirl
And a sit and a think
And a cheeky given wink,
With a tender loving kiss
And a grant of someone's wish
You can truly bring good cheer
To yourself and those held dear.

be Joy-full
x

Shirley is an artist, writer, entrepreneur and mother with a sweet and whimsical take on the world.

Using her unique style of painting and writing, and her team of trusted animal friends, she brings to light the finer qualities and quirks of what it means to be human with humour and grace.

www.shirleyharvey.com

www.ingramcontent.com/pod-product-compliance
Lightning Source LLC
LaVergne TN
LVHW071033070426
835507LV00003B/133